The Abolition of Slavery 1863

The Emancipation Proclamation

JANET RIEHECKY

Heinemann

H www.heinemann.co.uk/library
Visit our website to find out more information about Heinemann Library books.

To order:
☎ Phone 44 (0) 1865 888066
▤ Send a fax to 44 (0) 1865 314091
▢ Visit the Heinemann Bookshop at www.heinemann.co.uk/library to browse our catalogue and order online.

First published in Great Britain by Heinemann Library, Halley Court, Jordan Hill, Oxford OX2 8EJ, a division of Reed Educational and Professional Publishing Ltd. Heinemann is a registered trademark of Reed Educational & Professional Publishing Ltd.

OXFORD MELBOURNE AUCKLAND JOHANNESBURG BLANTYRE
GABORONE IBADAN PORTSMOUTH NH (USA) CHICAGO

Produced for Heinemann Library by Discovery Books Limited
Designed by Sabine Beaupré
Illustrations by Stefan Chabluk
Originated by Ambassador Litho Limited
Printed in Hong Kong

06 05 04 03   06 05 04 03
10 9 8 7 6 5 4 3 2   10 9 8 7 6 5 4 3 2 1

ISBN 0 431 06937 9 (hardback)   ISBN 0 431 06943 3 (paperback)

British Library Cataloguing in Publication Data

Riehecky, Janet
  The abolition of slavery 1863: the emancipation proclamation.
  - (Turning points in history)
  1. Slavery - History - Juvenile literature
  I. Title
  306.3'62'09

Northamptonshire Libraries & Information Service	
Peters	07-Aug-03
326	£6.50

Acknowledgements
The Publishers would like to thank the following for permission to reproduce photographs:
Corbis, pp. 5, 6, 7, 8, 9, 10, 11, 12, 13, 14, 15, 16, 17, 18, 20, 21, 22, 23, 24, 25, 26, 27, 28, 29;
The Granger Collection, p. 4.

Cover photographs reproduced with permission of *Corbis*.

Every effort has been made to contact copyright holders of any material reproduced in this book. Any omissions will be rectified in subsequent printings if notice is given to the Publisher.

Contents

Any words appearing in the text in bold, **like this**, are explained in the Glossary.

The president's proclamation

On 1 January 1863, President Abraham Lincoln walked into his office in the White House in the USA capital Washington, DC. On his desk was a document called the **Emancipation** Proclamation, a declaration of freedom. The document said that slaves would be freed in the southern states that were **rebelling** against the **Union**.

Lincoln picked up a pen, dipped it in ink, and began to sign it. As he did, his hand began to tremble. Did he have doubts about signing it? Not at all. He had just come from a reception where he had been shaking people's hands for three hours. His arm was tired. As he scrawled his full name at the bottom, he stated, 'I never, in my life, felt more certain that I was doing right than I do in signing this paper.'

By the President of the United States of America:

A Proclamation.

Whereas, on the twenty-second day of September, in the year of our Lord one thousand eight hundred and sixty-two, a proclamation was issued by the President of the United States, containing, among other things, the following, to wit:

"That on the first day of January, in the "year of our Lord one thousand eight hundred "and sixty-three, all persons held as slaves within "any State or designated part of a State, the people "whereof shall then be in rebellion against the "United States, shall be then, thenceforward, and "forever free; and the Executive Government of the "United States, including the military and naval "authority thereof, will recognize and maintain "the freedom of such persons, and will do no act "or acts to repress such persons, or any of them, "in any efforts they may make for their actual "freedom.

"That the Executive will, on the first day "of January aforesaid, by proclamation, designate "the States and parts of States, if any, in which the

This is the first page of the original four-page Emancipation Proclamation, handwritten by President Lincoln.

Rejoice!

In another part of Washington, DC, Henry Turner, a church minister, waited with a crowd at the office of the *Evening Star* newspaper. As the copies of the Proclamation came off the press, everyone grabbed for one. Turner captured the third copy and ran through the streets to his church. He described what happened next:

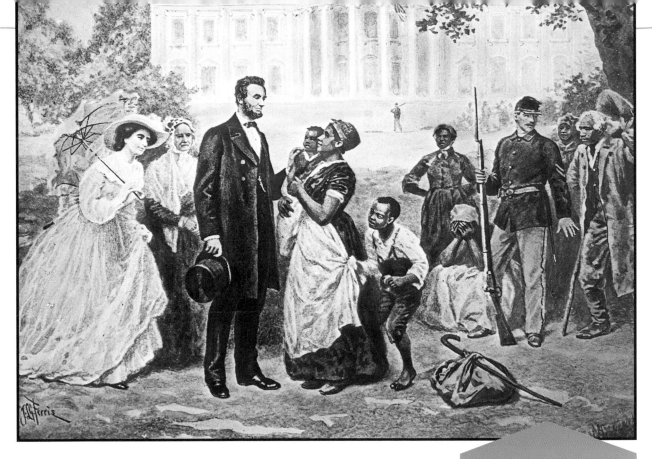

'When the people saw me coming with the paper in my hand, they raised a shouting cheer . . . I started to read the proclamation [but] I was out of breath and could not read. Mr Hinton, to whom I handed the paper, read it with great force and clearness . . . Men squealed, women fainted, dogs barked, white and colored people shook hands, songs were sung. . . . Great processions of colored and white men marched to and fro and congratulated President Lincoln on his proclamation . . . It was indeed a time of times . . . nothing like it will ever be seen again in this life.'

President Lincoln greets African Americans outside the White House on 1 January 1863. Black people all over the USA celebrated the announcement that slaves would be freed.

First step to freedom

The Emancipation Proclamation was made during the Civil War, a war between the northern and southern states of the USA. It declared freedom only for the slaves in states that had rebelled against the Union. But it was the first step toward ending the evil of slavery.

Slavery in the USA

In the beginning

Slavery was part of life in North America from almost the first days of the American **colonies**. In 1619, John Rolfe, a British settler in Jamestown, Virginia, bought 20 African slaves to work on his tobacco **plantation**. This was the first known sale of African slaves in what would become the USA. There were already thousands of African slaves in Central and South America, brought there by settlers from Portugal and Spain.

Where did the slaves come from?

European sailors traded with the kingdoms along the west coast of Africa. They offered goods – such as cloth, guns, tools and alcohol – for slaves. When this didn't provide enough slaves, they raided African villages. The Africans destined for slavery in America came from many different groups, such as the Yoruba, the Konga and the Fulani. They brought with them their varied traditions and languages.

Slaves were brought mostly from the west coast of Africa. Ships from New England would carry rum and other goods to Africa to trade for slaves. The slaves would be taken to the West Indies and traded for molasses, which would be taken to New England and made into more rum. This was called the Triangular Trade.

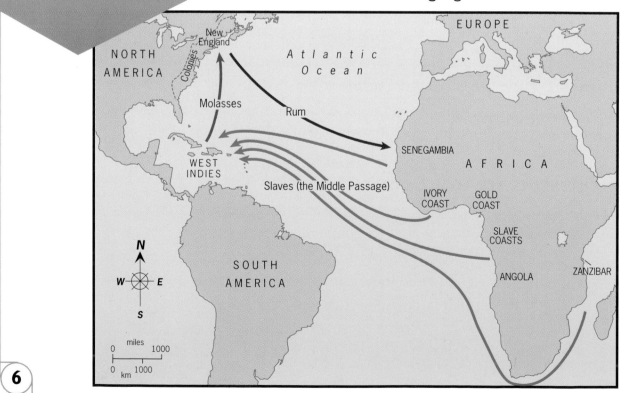

No independence for slaves

When the USA fought for its freedom from the British in 1776, many people thought that should mean freedom for slaves, too. But the southern states insisted that slavery remain legal. There were about 40,000 slaves in the North, or northern states. But there were more than 650,000 in the South, or southern states, where huge plantations kept large numbers of labourers busy all year round. By the time of the **Emancipation** Proclamation, the number of slaves in the South had grown to more than 3.5 million.

A group of slaves sits on the dock at Jamestown, Virginia, having just arrived from Africa on a slave ship. They would soon be sold to a plantation owner.

THE MIDDLE PASSAGE

As many Africans as possible were crammed into the holds of slave ships for the long weeks of the voyage known as the Middle Passage. On most ships they were nearly starved and kept in filthy conditions. Many would be chained or branded with a hot iron. Between ten and 40 per cent of them might die during the voyage. A rare first-hand account of the Middle Passage is that of Olaudah Equiano, kidnapped from his village in Nigeria when he was a child. In 1789 Equiano wrote an autobiography that brought people's attention to the horrors of slavery. Describing the Middle Passage, he said, *'The shrieks of the women and the groans of the dying rendered the whole scene a horror almost inconceivable.'*

Division between North and South

Differing lifestyles

In the mid-1800s, most people in the USA still lived on farms. But in the North, many people were moving into cities, producing goods in factories for their living. As the North became more and more **industrialized**, it became richer.

This painting shows slaves at work harvesting and processing cotton. Slaves worked in all kinds of jobs, but most were labourers on the large cotton and tobacco **plantations** of the South.

Many northerners saw slavery as morally wrong. Some slaves in the North were freed. But as long as its economy and lifestyle depended on slave labour, the South was not about to give it up. Wealthy southerners believed it was their right to own slaves. Even poor white southerners who didn't own slaves supported the system. As long as there were slaves, the poor whites wouldn't be at the bottom of the social order.

A slave's life

Being a slave meant being the property of another person, just like a piece of furniture. Southern slaves usually lived in shacks with dirt floors. They were given little food and often grew their own. They got up at dawn, worked until sunset and were whipped for any disobedience. It was actually against the law to teach a slave to read or write. Even worse, their owners could sell them, breaking up families and taking children from their parents.

Dreams of freedom

Before the **Emancipation** Proclamation, generations of slave families were kept in captivity, ignorance and misery with no hope of change. But a longing for freedom grew in the hearts of some slaves. Some sought to escape to the North. Others rose in **rebellion**. White southerners were terrified of rebellion and reacted brutally. In 1831, when the slave Nat Turner organized a rebellion, at least 100 innocent slaves were killed by slave owners in response.

Blacks in the North

Life wasn't easy for free blacks in the North either. Few white northerners thought that blacks should have equality with whites even if they disagreed with slavery. Some free blacks managed to prosper, but most were confined to **menial** jobs and **segregated** from whites. If they were caught without the papers that said they were free, they could be sold back into slavery.

A great horror of slave life was the auction block. There, slaves such as this family in Charleston, South Carolina, were displayed to be examined and then sold to the highest bidder. A family was often separated and its members sold to different owners.

The fight against slavery

First moves to ban slavery

Most people didn't think much about the rights and wrongs of slavery before the late eighteenth century. The debates that led to independence from the British, however, planted ideas about freedom that would not go away. By the early 1800s, most northern states had banned slavery. The international slave trade – the bringing of slaves from abroad – was banned in 1808. But slavery itself was still legal.

Another reason that slavery became an issue in the nineteenth century was that the USA was growing. The nation was acquiring and settling more **territories** across North America, and some of these territories were entering the **Union** – meaning joining the USA – as states. **Congress** needed to make decisions about whether or not to allow slavery to spread.

In 1828, a young journalist named William Lloyd Garrison decided to devote his life to ending slavery. In 1831, he began publishing the *Liberator*, a weekly newspaper dedicated to equal rights.

The abolitionists

The early 1800s saw the start of an organized **abolitionist** movement. Abolitionists preached that slavery was a sin against God. In 1833, the influential American Anti-Slavery Society was formed. The society produced literature, and sent speakers out to lecture about the cruelties inflicted on slaves. It pressured religious and political leaders to take up the cause.

Influential voices

One important abolitionist was Frederick Douglass, an escaped slave. His fluent arguments and powerful character convinced many people that slavery was evil. Another strong voice was that of Sojourner Truth. Despite never receiving any formal education, she inspired others with her dynamic personality and speeches against slavery.

Sojourner Truth had been born a slave in New York and was freed when that state banned slavery in 1828. Like many abolitionists, she was deeply religious. Truth believed God had called her to fight for equality for slaves and women.

UNCLE TOM'S CABIN

In 1852 a book by Harriet Beecher Stowe, called *Uncle Tom's Cabin*, was published. Although it was a work of fiction, it was so moving that many white people faced up to the reality of slavery for first time. The story of the brave slave Eliza who saved her son's life, and the gentle, loyal Uncle Tom who died at the hands of his owner, brought support to the abolitionists. It is said that when Harriet Beecher Stowe visited Abraham Lincoln in the White House during the Civil War, he greeted her with, *'So you're the little lady who started this great big war.'*

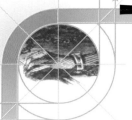

The division grows

The Missouri Compromise

In 1820, there were eleven slave states (in the South) and eleven free states (in the North) in the **Union**.

Because the **territory** of Missouri wanted to join as a slave state, Congressman Henry Clay from Kentucky suggested a compromise. Missouri could be a slave state, but Maine would be admitted as a free state, keeping a balance between North and South. The Missouri Compromise also said that any new states south of the **latitude line** 36°30' would join the Union as slave states. North of that line, slaves would be free.

More disputes

The Missouri Compromise line didn't apply to the territories in the West, however. In the following years, there were many arguments between North and South about the spread of slavery into the West. In 1850, again with the help of Henry Clay, **Congress** worked out another compromise.

One of the most influential politicians in the history of the USA was Henry Clay. He was involved in most important decisions from the early 1800s, and he worked on both the Missouri Compromise and the Compromise of 1850.

In addition to settling the dispute over the western territories, the Compromise of 1850 included two new laws. One, to please the North, made the buying and selling of slaves in Washington, DC, illegal. The other, to please the South, was called the **Fugitive** Slave Law. This new law said that anyone who refused to help capture escaped slaves could be punished. Nobody was very pleased, however, and northerners and southerners continued their bitter disputes about slavery as more territories became states.

The Dred Scott decision

Dred Scott was a slave from Virginia who had been taken by his owner to Illinois and Wisconsin Territory. After his master died, Scott claimed in the United States **Supreme Court** that he should be freed because he had lived for five years in those free areas. But the Supreme Court ruled that blacks had no rights at all because they were not citizens. It also ruled that it was **unconstitutional** for Congress to pass laws, such as the Missouri Compromise, prohibiting slavery anywhere. The Dred Scott decision divided the country even more.

One 'conductor' on the Underground Railroad was the former slave Harriet Tubman (left). Tubman helped more than 300 slaves escape and stated proudly that she never lost a 'passenger'.

THE UNDERGROUND RAILROAD

A number of **abolitionists** defied the Fugitive Slave Law and risked punishment by helping slaves escape. The Underground Railroad was not underground, nor was it a railroad. It was a secret organization of people who helped escaped slaves to get from the South to the North. They provided places to rest and help from one 'station' to the next.

The election of 1860

Desperate measures

After the Dred Scott decision, some **abolitionists** began taking the law into their own hands. In 1859, abolitionist John Brown raided an **arsenal** in Virginia, planning to get weapons to arm slaves. He and his followers were caught and executed. But the episode added to the fears of white southerners who were convinced that abolitionists were going to take away their slaves.

A Republican president

As the election of 1860 approached, the two political parties that competed to run the country had to choose their **candidates** for the presidency. Northerners and southerners in the Democratic party could not agree on their ideas about slavery. The party split, and ended up with two presidential candidates. The Republican party, which opposed the spread of slavery, chose Abraham Lincoln, a former lawyer and one of their party leaders.

After the outbreak of war, four more states seceded from the Union, bringing the total to eleven. Only four slave states, known as the border states, chose to stay loyal to the North. A large section of Virginia refused to secede, and it became the state of West Virginia in 1863.

Union states

Confederate states

State admitted to the Union, 1863

Border states

United States territories

Confederates opened fire on Fort Sumter with cannons from the shore. You can see the cannonballs landing and exploding inside the fort in this picture. After a two-day bombardment, the fort surrendered.

With the Democratic vote split between North and South, Abraham Lincoln was elected easily. He said that he would not interfere with slavery where it already existed. But the South didn't believe him. In December 1860, before Lincoln was even **inaugurated**, South Carolina **seceded** from the **Union**.

The Confederate States of America

Six other states soon followed. They formed a new union of states called the 'Confederate States of America'. Statesman Jefferson Davis was chosen as their first president. Lincoln declared that states could not secede from the Union and vowed not to tolerate any act of violence against the USA. But on 12 April 1861 Confederates, also called '**Rebels**', attacked Fort Sumter in South Carolina. Lincoln answered by gathering an army. The Civil War had begun.

LINCOLN AND SLAVERY

President Lincoln made no secret of his personal view that slavery was wrong. But he said, '*My paramount object in this struggle is to save the Union, and is not either to save or to destroy slavery.*' Lincoln said that if he could reunite the country by keeping slavery, he would. He also realized most northerners wouldn't support the Civil War if it was being fought to free slaves. But as the war progressed, Lincoln changed his mind. He became convinced that slavery was such an evil that the war could not be won unless it was abolished.

A reason to fight

The Civil War begins

When the Civil War began, both sides believed they would win quickly and easily. The first major battle, the First Battle of Bull Run in Virginia in July 1861, was a shock to both sides, but especially to the North which lost the battle. Almost 900 men were killed in the fighting, and it was suddenly clear that the war could be long and bloody.

Lincoln (third from left) discussed the Emancipation Proclamation with his **cabinet** in July 1862. Most cabinet members agreed it wasn't yet time to make the announcement.

A shift in attitude

The Confederates continued to win battles. At the same time, more Americans were becoming convinced that slavery was evil. Many, including President Lincoln, saw a practical as well as moral advantage to freeing slaves in the South. The work of slaves helped support the Confederate Army. A proclamation freeing slaves could remove that support from the **Rebels** and give it to the **Union**. It would also win the support of the UK and France because both countries were firmly against slavery.

Lincoln decides about emancipation

Lincoln was becoming convinced that this was really a war over slavery, but he worried about what the border states would do if slaves were freed. If the border states went over to the Confederacy, that added strength might be enough to defeat the Union.

Lincoln reached a decision. He would free only the slaves in areas controlled by the Rebels. Lincoln

waited for a suitable moment. On 22 September 1862, he issued a Preliminary **Emancipation** Proclamation. It stated that, unless the Confederate states returned to the Union before 1 January 1863, all their slaves would be 'then, thenceforward, and forever free'.

FIRST STEPS TO EMANCIPATION

During the Civil War, **Congress** passed several laws that led up to the Emancipation Proclamation:

July 1861	The First **Confiscation** Act said that slaves engaged in work that helped the Rebels could be seized by the Union
March 1862	Military personnel were prohibited from returning **fugitive** slaves to their owners
10 April 1862	Compensation was offered to owners who freed their slaves
16 April 1862	Slavery was abolished in the District of Columbia (the area around the US capital city of Washington)
June 1862	Slavery was prohibited in all US **territories**
July 1862	All slaves whose owners supported the Confederacy were declared free

Union forces pour across Antietam Creek to attack the Confederates in the Battle of Antietam in 1862. When the Rebels withdrew, it was not a great victory for the Union. But it was important, because until then the South had looked much stronger than the North. The Rebel retreat gave Lincoln the advantage he needed to make his Preliminary Emancipation Proclamation.

The Proclamation

Lincoln frees the slaves

In the **Emancipation** Proclamation, Lincoln named the areas it applied to and pronounced the slaves in those areas to be free. He advised freed slaves to refrain from violence except in self-defence, and to 'labor faithfully for reasonable wages'. He also welcomed them into the **Union** armed forces. The document ended by asking for God's blessing.

Reaction in the North

In the North, thousands of people poured into the streets to celebrate. They sang songs, held parades and gave speeches. Not everyone was glad. **Prejudice** against blacks existed in the North. And some **abolitionists** wanted slavery abolished in the Union states, too.

Reaction in the South

Although slave owners did not tell their slaves about the Proclamation, many learned of it anyway. Escapes increased and more slaves rose up in rebellion. Slaves were not immediately freed because of the Proclamation. But a blow for freedom had been struck. The document stated to all the world that ending slavery was the goal of the Civil War.

This painting, although not showing a real event, celebrates the Emancipation Proclamation. The woman in the carriage is a symbol of freedom, and President Lincoln is on the right, holding the Proclamation. In the background is the Capitol building, seat of the US government.

THE EMANCIPATION PROCLAMATION

Whereas on the 22nd day of September, AD 1862, a proclamation was issued by the President of the United States, containing, among other things, the following, to wit:

'That on the 1st day of January, AD 1863, all persons held as slaves within any State or designated part of a State the people whereof shall then be in **rebellion** against the United States shall be then, thenceforward, and forever free; and the executive government of the United States, including the military and naval authority thereof, will recognize and maintain the freedom of such persons and will do no act or acts to repress such persons, or any of them, in any efforts they may make for their actual freedom.

'That the executive will on the 1st day of January aforesaid, by proclamation, designate the States and parts of States, if any, in which the people thereof, respectively, shall then be in rebellion against the United States; and the fact that any State or the people thereof shall on that day be in good faith represented in the **Congress** of the United States by members chosen thereto at elections wherein a majority of the qualified voters of such States shall have participated shall, in the absence of strong countervailing testimony, be deemed conclusive evidence that such State and the people thereof are not then in rebellion against the United States.'

Now, therefore, I, Abraham Lincoln, President of the United States, by virtue of the power in me vested as Commander-In-Chief of the Army and Navy of the United States in time of actual armed rebellion against the authority and government of the United States, and as a fit and necessary war measure for suppressing said rebellion, do, on this 1st day of January, AD 1863, and in accordance with my purpose so to do, publicly proclaimed for the full period of one hundred days from the first day above mentioned, order and designate as the States and parts of States wherein the people thereof, respectively, are this day in rebellion against the United States the following, to wit: Arkansas, Texas, Louisiana (except the parishes of St. Bernard, Palquemines, Jefferson, St. John, St. Charles, St. James, Ascension, Assumption, Terrebone, Lafourche, St. Mary, St. Martin, and Orleans, including the city of New Orleans), Mississippi, Alabama, Florida, Georgia, South Carolina, North Carolina, and Virginia (except the forty-eight counties designated as West Virginia, and also the counties of Berkley, Accomac, Northampton, Elizabeth City, York, Princess Ann, and Norfolk, including the cities of Norfolk and Portsmouth), and which excepted parts are for the present left precisely as if this proclamation were not issued. And by virtue of the power and for the purpose aforesaid, I do order and declare that all persons held as slaves within said designated States and parts of States are, and henceforward shall be, free; and that the Executive Government of the United States, including the military and naval authorities thereof, will recognize and maintain the freedom of said persons. And I hereby enjoin upon the people so declared to be free to abstain from all violence, unless in necessary self-defence; and I recommend to them that, in all case when allowed, they labor faithfully for reasonable wages. And I further declare and make known that such persons of suitable condition will be received into the armed service of the United States to garrison forts, positions, stations, and other places, and to man vessels of all sorts in said service. And upon this act, sincerely believed to be an act of justice, warranted by the **Constitution** upon military necessity, I invoke the considerate judgment of mankind and the gracious favor of Almighty God.

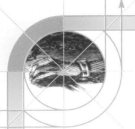

Emancipation begins

The end of the war

During 1863 and 1864, the tide of the Civil War turned. The **Union** forces of the North, under the leadership of General Ulysses S Grant, were able to defeat the Confederate forces of the South. On 9 April 1865, Confederate General Robert E Lee surrendered to Grant. The Civil War was over.

Assassination

Lincoln's plans for reuniting the nation included the abolition of slavery in the entire country. Slaves were to receive full rights as citizens, including voting and holding **public office**. How far these plans might have got remains unknown. On 15 April 1865, six days after the end of the Civil War, Lincoln died after being shot by John Wilkes Booth. Vice President Andrew Johnson took over the presidency.

As a result of the Emancipation Proclamation, thousands of former slaves in the South headed north, both to find freedom and to support the Union in the Civil War.

New rights

The **Emancipation** Proclamation had been issued as a war measure to help defeat the South. Because of this, it couldn't become law in the rest of the nation without an **amendment** to the **Constitution**. Instead, **Congress** passed three amendments to ensure the rights of African Americans. The Thirteenth Amendment in 1865 banned slavery anywhere in the USA. (The Emancipation Proclamation had only freed slaves in the **Rebel** states.) The Fourteenth Amendment in 1868 made it illegal to deprive any citizen of life, liberty or property unless the law allowed it. It said every citizen was entitled to equal protection under the law. The Fifteenth Amendment in 1870 said it was against the law to deny any man the right to vote on the basis of race, colour or previous slavery.

A US infantry unit stands at ease during the Civil War. More than 180,000 African Americans served as soldiers in the war, and 38,000 were killed in the fighting.

AFRICAN AMERICAN SOLDIERS

The wording of the Emancipation Proclamation was a clear invitation for blacks to join the Union Army. They did by the thousands, both escaped slaves and freed men from the North. Most were at first put to work doing **menial** labour, but others were trained as soldiers. One of the most famous black regiments was the 54th Massachusetts Infantry. Many white northern soldiers had not wanted to serve alongside black soldiers. They thought blacks would be cowardly and that they just weren't clever enough to handle the job. The outstanding bravery and ability of the 54th Massachusetts proved them wrong and helped pave the way for equality for blacks.

Reconstruction

Rebuilding the nation

After the war, the USA entered a period known as Reconstruction, meaning 'rebuilding'. This term reflected a need to reunite the nation, but also to rebuild American society so that there was a place for millions of newly freed black people.

The government realized that former slaves would need help adjusting to their new lives. So **Congress** established the Bureau of Refugees, Freedmen, and Abandoned Lands (known usually as the Freedmen's Bureau) to provide help. The Freedmen's Bureau provided food, temporary shelter, clothing and medical care. Its projects were not always run well, but they did provide some badly needed assistance.

Political Reconstruction

During Reconstruction, there were many disagreements within the **federal** government. President Johnson was from the southern state of Tennessee and had more sympathy for white

The Freedmen's Bureau only existed between 1865 and 1872. But it founded over 4000 schools to help freed slaves – both adults and children – learn to read, write and do arithmetic. This photograph from the 1860s shows one of the Freedmen schools in Beaufort, South Carolina.

southerners than for former slaves. He tried to prevent Congress from extending citizenship to blacks. Congress fought back, however, and in 1866 passed the **Civil Rights** Act, which declared black people to be American citizens.

Starting in 1867, Congress passed other laws, called the Reconstruction Acts, that forced state governments in the South to recognize the rights of African Americans. For the first time, black people voted and took **public office**.

During Reconstruction, hundreds of African American men became government officials, and eighteen became Congressmen. The first black members of Congress are seen here. The group includes Hiram Revels (far left), a church leader who became the USA's first black senator in 1870.

The end of Reconstruction

Reconstruction governments in the South worked hard to rebuild the economy and improve life for their many new citizens. Within a few short years, however, Reconstruction was over. The Republicans still held power in the national government. But by 1877, white Democrats regained control of southern state governments, and much of the work towards equality was undone.

CARPETBAGGERS

Many northerners went south during Reconstruction. Some intended to help the newly freed slaves. Others hoped to take advantage of the South's problems. Southerners disliked all of them, and called them 'carpetbaggers' because some northerners arrived with their belongings in suitcases made from carpet. A few carpetbaggers grabbed all the power and money they could get. Most, however, came to teach, advise and help in the rebuilding of the South.

A segregated society

Jim Crow laws

The white, southern Democrats who regained control at a local level after Reconstruction were as determined as ever to deny rights to black people. By the early 1900s, they had succeeded in creating a **segregated** society in the South. Many southern states passed laws, known as Jim Crow laws. (The name came from a fictional character who was an old black slave.) Whites and blacks were required to use separate schools and separate hospitals. Churches, restaurants and transport systems were segregated, too. So were many shops and cinemas.

A white man and a black man drink from their own sides of a segregated water fountain. A hundred years after slaves were freed, there were still signs all over the south reading 'Colored Only' and 'Whites Only'.

SHARECROPPERS

After the Emancipation Proclamation, some southern blacks were able to find work as sharecroppers. Sharecropping was a system in which white landowners provided living quarters and supplies to workers in exchange for a share of the crops raised. Often, landowners took so much that the sharecroppers were no better off than they had been as slaves.

Voting rights denied

The **Emancipation** Proclamation may have ended slavery, but whites still held the power in southern society. They did everything they could to prevent African Americans from gaining an equal place in society. Despite the Fifteenth **Amendment**, they found several ways to keep blacks from voting. For example, in some places, local laws stated that only people who could read and write could vote. Few former slaves could read or write, and so they were prevented from voting.

Separate but equal

Even the courts upheld the Jim Crow laws. In 1892, Homer Plessy was arrested for sitting in a 'whites only' railway carriage. He was found guilty of violating segregation laws. Plessy appealed to the US **Supreme Court**, saying he was entitled to equal protection under the Fourteenth Amendment. In 1896, in a ruling known as *Plessy vs Ferguson*, the Supreme Court declared that separate facilities were legal as long as they were equal. They rarely were equal, of course, but this was hard to prove in court.

A secret, terrorist organization called the Ku Klux Klan was formed in 1866 to keep black people from voting and so keep the whites in power. The Klan wore hooded robes and used burning crosses to frighten victims. They attacked and murdered African Americans and burned down homes, churches and schools.

The fight for equality

The NAACP

In spite of the **Emancipation** Proclamation, black citizens were still denied equal opportunities in the USA. In 1909, a group formed the National Association for the Advancement of Colored People (NAACP) to challenge **segregation** laws in the courts. They won several victories and forced the public to acknowledge the lack of progress made since the Emancipation Proclamation.

One the NAACP's biggest victories was in education. In 1954, the Supreme Court said that schools had to be desegregated. When a white community in Little Rock, Arkansas, refused to comply, President Eisenhower sent in soldiers so that black students could enter the school with protection.

Falling barriers

World War II helped to lower some barriers as black soldiers once again proved their bravery and skill. After the war, President Harry Truman ordered the armed forces to **desegregate**. Baseball player Jackie Robinson was signed up by the Brooklyn Dodgers, the first time an African American had entered professional sports. And then in 1954, the **Supreme Court** ruled that 'separate but equal facilities are [by their nature] unequal'.

The civil rights movement

Most people date the beginning of the **civil rights** movement to December 1955, when Rosa Parks was arrested in Montgomery, Alabama, for refusing to give up her seat on the bus to a white person. Martin Luther King, Jnr, at the time a young church minister, organized a **boycott** of the city's buses. For more than a year African Americans refused to ride the buses. This non-violent protest achieved victory when the Supreme Court declared that Montgomery's bus segregation laws were **unconstitutional**.

Spurred on by this success, Dr King and other civil rights leaders took this crusade throughout the South. They succeeded in gaining job opportunities and fair treatment from many businesses. In the 1960s, public opinion shifted in favour of the movement, and President John F Kennedy gave his support to equal rights. Later, **Congress** passed the Civil Rights Act of 1964, banning segregation in the USA.

Martin Luther King, Jnr, (front row wearing hat) marches with his wife Coretta in 1965. Marches and other non-violent demonstrations were the backbone of the 1960s civil rights movement.

WE SHALL OVERCOME

The American folk song 'We Shall Overcome' became the anthem of the civil rights movement. It took its words from a 1901 hymn:
'We shall overcome, we shall overcome,
we shall overcome some day.
Oh, deep in my heart, I do believe
we shall overcome some day.'

Room for change

Equal opportunity?

In 1965, **Congress** passed the Voting Rights Act, which struck down the Jim Crow laws that had restricted blacks' right to vote. It had taken more than a hundred years since the **Emancipation** Proclamation for blacks to achieve legal equality with whites. But did the Emancipation Proclamation really bring about social equality for the descendants of African slaves?

It would appear not. In the USA poverty is still more widespread among blacks than among whites. In 1991, the overall family income for African Americans was only 57 per cent of that of white families. And **prejudice** still exists. African Americans are subjected to insult and some whites try to keep blacks out of their shops, their clubs or their neighbourhoods. Black people are not highly visible in senior positions at work. African Americans are more likely to be arrested and convicted of crimes than whites, and their prison sentences are usually more severe. There is still need for change.

In poor, black, urban communities it can still seem as if there are differing opportunities depending on the colour of your skin. Frustration at racial inequality erupted into riots in Los Angeles, California, in 1992. These people are watching their neighbourhood burn after attacks on buildings during the riots.

An enriched culture

The USA has benefitted as African Americans rediscover their **heritage**. Slaves brought from Africa were forbidden to follow any of their customs. Emancipation turned that around. African art, music and dance have inspired African Americans and now play a part in American culture.

Secretary of State Colin Powell (left) takes his oath of office in January 2001 while President George W Bush and Mrs Powell watch. Powell, a former general and war hero, is admired for his bravery, wisdom and efforts to improve social conditions for whites and blacks.

American society as a whole is also richer because of the fight by African Americans to achieve equality. All Americans can admire the skill of black sports stars, such as Tiger Woods, or the leadership of politicians such as Colin Powell. Women, Native Americans and other groups have been inspired to fight for their own rights because of what African Americans achieved. Gaining true equality is a long, difficult road, but each step brings the dream closer. The Emancipation Proclamation was an important step in achieving this dream.

KWANZAA

The holiday Kwanzaa was created in 1966 by Dr Maulana Karenga, a college professor who wanted to help African Americans preserve their African heritage. Kwanzaa is a week-long celebration based on traditional African harvest festivals. Each day the participants focus on one of seven principles. These are unity, **self-determination**, collective work and responsibility, co-operative economics, purpose, creativity and faith.

Time-line

1619	First slaves sold in the American Colonies
1787	Northwest Ordinance prohibits slavery in Northwest Territory
1789	Constitution makes slavery legal in USA
1808	1 January – USA prohibits importation of slaves
1820–21	Missouri Compromise passed
1831	William Lloyd Garrison begins publishing the *Liberator*
1833	American Anti-Slavery Society formed
1850	Compromise of 1850 including Fugitive Slave Law passed
	Buying and selling of slaves banned in Washington, DC
1852	*Uncle Tom's Cabin* published
1854	Republican Party formed
1857	Supreme Court decides on case of Dred Scott
1859	16 October – John Brown leads raid on federal arsenal
1860	Abraham Lincoln elected president
	20 December – South Carolina secedes from Union
1861	February – Rebel states form Confederate States of America
	12 April – Confederates bombard Fort Sumter
	21 July – First Battle of Bull Run
	July – First Confiscation Act
1862	March – Military personnel prohibited from returning fugitive slaves to their owners
	10 April – Compensation offered to owners freeing slaves
	16 April – Slavery abolished in District of Columbia
	June – Slavery prohibited in all US territories
	17 September – Battle of Antietam
	22 September – Preliminary Emancipation Proclamation
1863	1 January – Emancipation Proclamation goes into effect
1865	9 April – Confederate surrender brings end to Civil War
	14 April – President Lincoln shot (died 15 April)
	Reconstruction period begins
	18 December – Thirteenth Amendment approved
1866	Civil Rights Act passed
	Ku Klux Klan formed
1867	First Reconstruction Act passed
1868	Fourteenth Amendment approved
1870	Fifteenth Amendment approved
1877	Reconstruction period ends
1896	*Plessy vs Ferguson* establishes principle of 'separate but equal'
1909	NAACP formed
1954	Supreme Court rules against segregation
1964	Civil Rights Act of 1964 passed
1965	Voting Rights Act passed

Glossary

abolitionist	person committed to ending slavery
amendment	official change or added definition made to the Constitution of the United States of America
arsenal	collection of weapons
boycott	refusal to buy something or use something, as a protest
cabinet	group of statesmen who serve as advisors to the president
candidate	person seeking to be chosen for an official position or job
civil rights	basic rights of every person, such as freedom
colony	settlement, area or country controlled or owned by another nation
confiscation	seizure of goods by an official
Congress	government of the USA. A Congressman or woman is an elected member of Congress.
Constitution	document that states the basic principles and laws of the USA
desegregate	get rid of segregation
emancipation	setting free
federal	concerning the whole nation as opposed to separate states
fugitive	escaped person running away from authorities
heritage	something inherited from earlier generations that forms part of a person's culture, such as traditions, beliefs and language
inaugurate	place in office with official ceremony, such as the swearing-in ceremony for a president
industrialize	change from a society based mainly on farming and non-mechanical production to one based on use of machinery for mass production
latitude line	imaginary line going horizontally around Earth. Latitude lines are measured in degrees north or south of the equator and make it easier to locate particular places.
menial	low-ranking
paramount	most important
plantation	large farm where crops such as tobacco or cotton are grown and large numbers of people are employed as labourers
prejudice	judgement about something based on previously-held ideas rather than real reasons, for instance dislike of someone for their skin colour rather than for their actual qualities as a person
public office	position of authority in government or other public role
rebel	to fight against authority, law or control. People who do this are known as rebels and their actions are called rebellions. The Confederates were called 'Rebels' during the Civil War.
secede	leave or withdraw from a group
segregate	keep groups of people separate from each other
self-determination	having control of decisions and choices in one's own life
Supreme Court	the highest law court in the USA that has the power to make final decisions on legal matters
territory	areas of North America in the eighteenth century outside the actual states but owned and settled by the USA
unconstitutional	going against the rules and principles of the Constitution
Union	another name for the United States of America. When territories belonging to the USA became states, this was called 'joining the Union'.

Index